Author:

Kathryn Senior is a former biomedical research scientist who studied at Cambridge University for a degree and a doctorate in microbiology. After four years in research she joined the world of publishing as an editor of children's science books. She has now been a full-time science writer for 8 years. She is the author of several books, including **Rainforest** in the *Fast Forward* series and **Superbugs and Minibeasts** in the *Checkers* series.

Series creator:

David Salariya was born in Dundee, Scotland, where he studied illustration and printmaking. He has illustrated a wide range of books and has created many new series of books for publishers in the UK and overseas. In 1989 he established The Salariya Book Company. He lives in Brighton with his wife, the illustrator Shirley Willis, and their son.

© The Salariya Book Company Ltd MM

Created, designed and produced by
THE SALARIYA BOOK COMPANY LTD
25 Marlborough Place, Brighton BN1 1UB

Published in Great Britain in 2000 by Hodder Wayland, an imprint of Hodder Children's Books

A catalogue record for this book is available from the British Library

ISBN 07502 3153 X

Printed and bound in China

Hodder Children's Books
A division of Hodder Headline plc
338 Euston Road, London NW1 3BH

Additional artists:

Simon Calder

Bill Donohoe

Nick Hewetson

Lee Peters

Tony Townsend

Editor:

Karen Barker Smith

Editorial Assistant:

Stephanie Cole

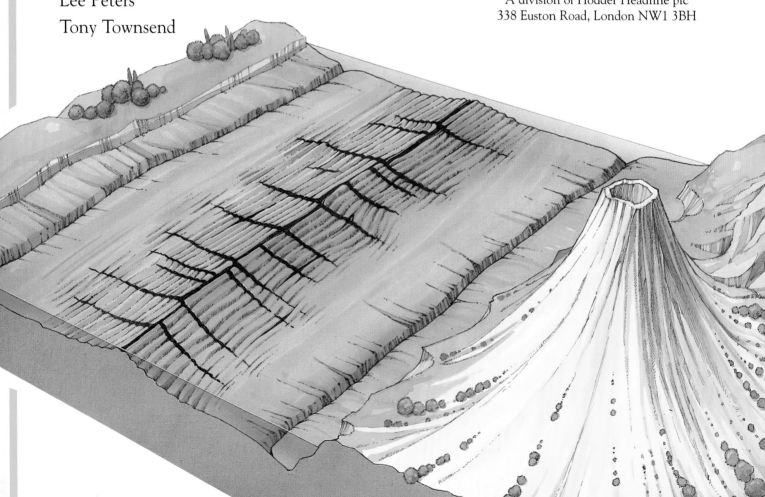

PLANET
EARTH

Written by
KATHRYN SENIOR

Illustrated by
DAVE ANTRAM
and
CAROLYN SCRACE

Created and designed by
DAVID SALARIYA

HODDER
Wayland

An imprint of Hodder Children's Books

Contents

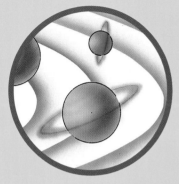

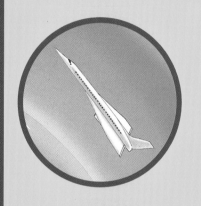

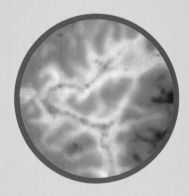

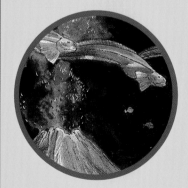

The Big Bang

The universe began with the Big Bang. This is the name given to a huge explosion that happened 15 billion years ago. In a split second, the universe expanded from almost nothing, a tiny dot smaller than a pinprick, into the vast expanse of space. The universe is still expanding – in the billions of years since the Big Bang, galaxies, solar systems, planets and moons have formed.

Our own planet, Earth, is one of the planets in the solar system that centres on our sun, a star that is part of the Milky Way. The Milky Way is a flat disc of stars which is part of a large galaxy. No one knows how many galaxies there are in the universe.

A galaxy is a group of stars, dust and gas. The spiral galaxy shown above is one of the most common types. It has coiled arms that spring out of a central nucleus. Elliptical galaxies, which look like flattened spheres, are also common. Irregular galaxies are those in which the stars have not formed into any regular shape. These are the rarest of all galaxies.

Our Place in the Universe

Our own galaxy is a complicated collection of stars, planets, dust and gas. It is a spiral galaxy that has a central nucleus containing older stars and several arms that spin out to form a disc. This disc contains younger stars, star clusters and spiral mini-galaxies and it is called the Milky Way. Our sun is about two-thirds of the way along one side of it. All the stars that we can see from Earth, at least 100 billion of them, are in the Milky Way. A spherical halo surrounds the whole galaxy and this is made up from older stars that group together in irregular lumps called globular clusters.

The sun (below) is the star around which Earth and the other planets in our solar system orbit. It is a shining mass of gas made of 74% hydrogen and 26% helium. In the core of the sun, the process of nuclear fission converts hydrogen to helium, releasing large amounts of energy as heat and radiation.

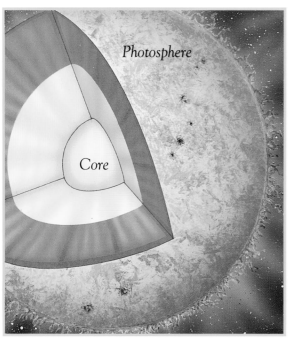

Photosphere

Core

The temperature at the sun's core is incredibly high (15 million° C) and the core is very dense. It is only one thousandth of the whole sun's volume. The rest of the sun, the photosphere, is mainly gas.

The sun

The sun is at the centre of our solar system and a collection of planets, satellites, comets, dust and debris orbit around it. The planets formed about 4.6 million years ago as debris and matter from space collected together and balls of gas and dust condensed to form rocky spheres. Many of the planets still show the scars from the impact of debris. Such collisions were 2,000 times more common 4 million years ago than they are now.

9

The planets of our solar system (in order of size)

1 Pluto
2 Mercury
3 Mars
4 Venus
5 Earth
6 Neptune
7 Uranus
8 Saturn
9 Jupiter

The outer planets Jupiter, Saturn, Uranus and Neptune all have large numbers of moons (Saturn has 18). These planets have metal cores but are surrounded by huge atmospheres full of swirling gas. Pluto is a very small planet that may have broken off from one of the larger planets. There may be a tenth planet, but we do not know much about this yet.

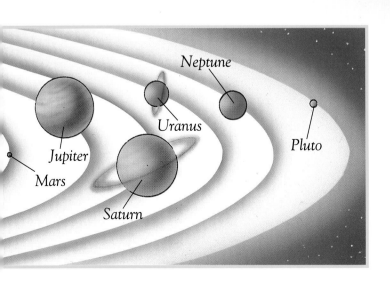

Neptune
Uranus
Pluto
Jupiter
Mars
Saturn

Between the planets Mars and Jupiter lies a deep band of rocky debris called the asteroid belt. Today, 3,500 major asteroids have been identified. The largest, Ceres, is over 1,000 kilometres (km) wide. There are also about 100 million smaller asteroids in the belt. Recent asteroids are thought to have formed when a group of minor planets with metal cores and rocky mantles broke up into small fragments.

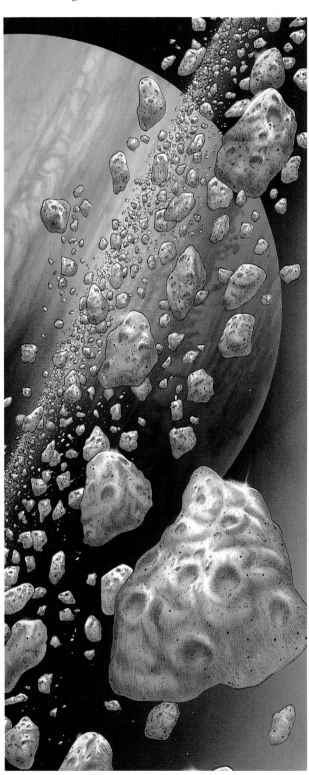

1.5 billion years ago

4.5 billion years ago

The moon (pictured above) is the only natural satellite of Earth. Its mass is 1.23% that of Earth and it has no atmosphere. Its surface is covered with mountains, craters and plains, which formed when the moon was bombarded with rocks about 4,500 million years ago. Intense heat in the centre of the moon caused some of the surface rock to melt, leaving lava pools that then solidified. These look like lakes but there is no evidence that running water has ever existed on the moon.

Planet Earth

Earth is the third planet from the sun in the solar system. It is a slightly flattened sphere that is approximately 12,800 km in diameter at the equator. Earth rotates completely once every 24 hours, giving us our day length. It takes 365 and a quarter days to orbit the sun, giving us our year. The extra day is made up in our calendar by adding an extra day to the end of February every four years. Earth's axis is tilted at an angle so the amount of heat that gets to the surface of the planet from the sun varies during the year. These variations create the seasons of spring, summer, autumn and winter.

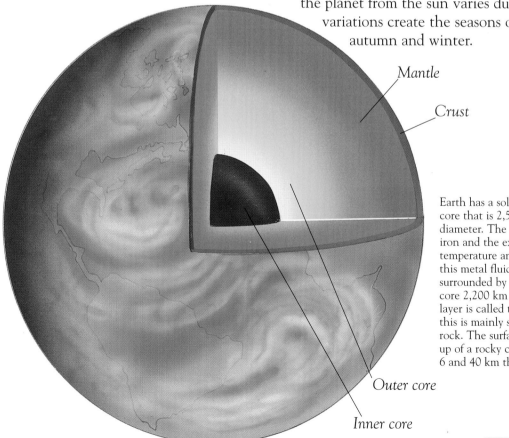

Mantle

Crust

Outer core

Inner core

Earth has a solid metal inner core that is 2,500 km in diameter. The core is 90% iron and the extremely high temperature and pressure keep this metal fluid. The core is surrounded by a liquid outer core 2,200 km thick. The next layer is called the mantle and this is mainly semi-molten rock. The surface is made up of a rocky crust between 6 and 40 km thick.

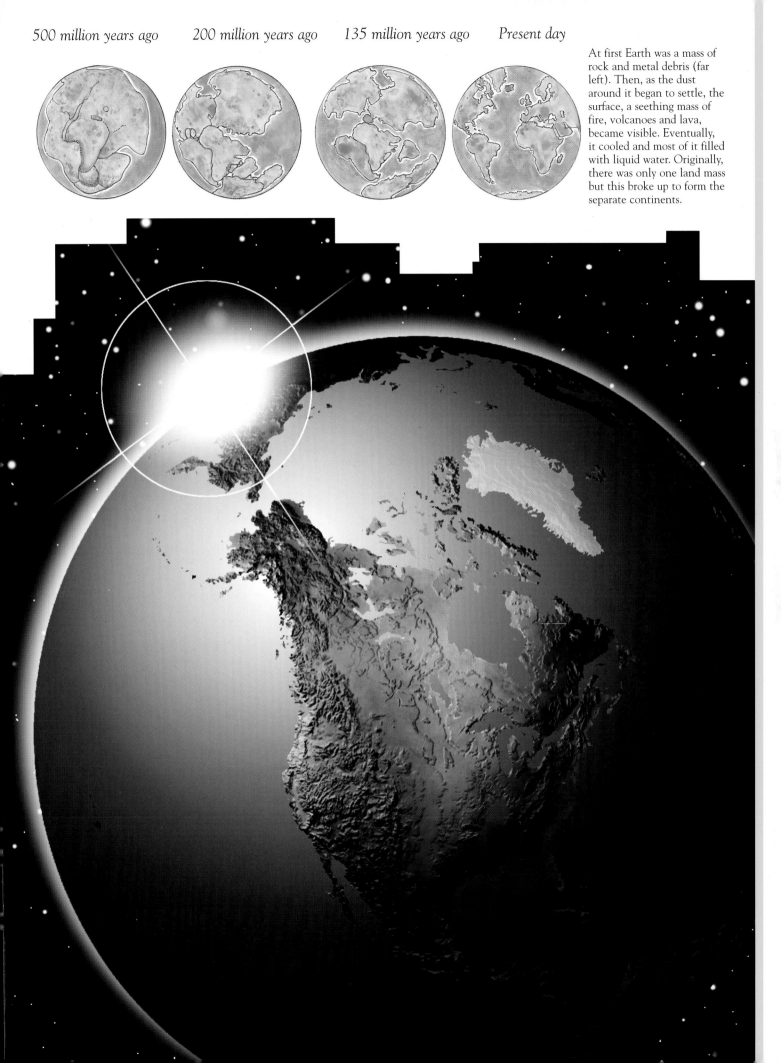

500 million years ago   200 million years ago   135 million years ago   Present day

At first Earth was a mass of rock and metal debris (far left). Then, as the dust around it began to settle, the surface, a seething mass of fire, volcanoes and lava, became visible. Eventually, it cooled and most of it filled with liquid water. Originally, there was only one land mass but this broke up to form the separate continents.

Coral reef

In the deep ocean trenches black smokers (right) create pockets of warm water, where bacteria multiply. A variety of creatures have evolved to feed on the bacteria, including the huge giant squid. This creature was thought to be a myth until dead ones were dredged out of the water off the coast of New Zealand in the 1980s.

Beneath the Oceans

About 71% of the planet's surface is covered by saltwater oceans called the Pacific, the Atlantic, the Indian, the Arctic and the Southern oceans. The fact that water exists on Earth in its liquid form is one of the main reasons why life evolved here. Without water, nothing can survive. Early life-forms such as bacteria and single-celled organisms evolved in the water and today the oceans are home to a huge variety of creatures. Rich ecosystems are found all around their shores and near the surface of the oceans. Recently, scientists have discovered that ocean trenches up to 11,000 m deep are also bursting with many weird and wonderful creatures. These deep sea areas are called the Abyssal zone.

Key to the abyssal zone

1. Rat tails
2. Deep sea shrimp
3. Deep sea anglers
4. Stalked crinoids
5. Brotulids
6. Deep sea eels
7. Gulpers
8. Black smoker (underwater volcano)

Abyssal zone

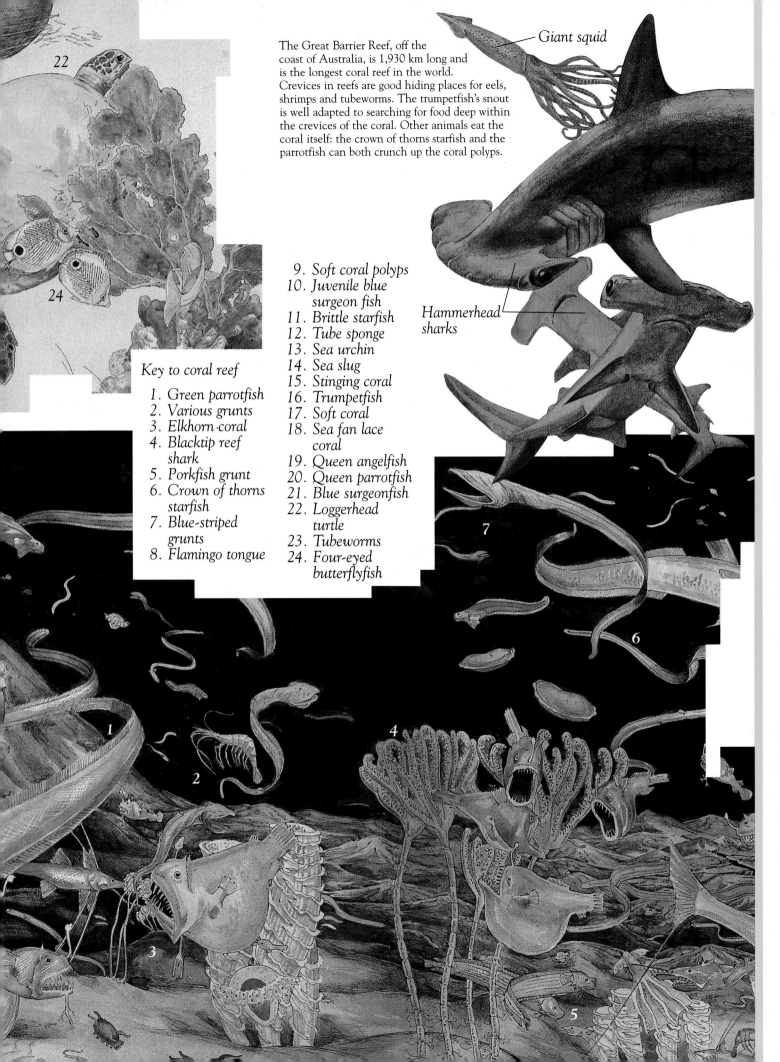

Giant squid

The Great Barrier Reef, off the coast of Australia, is 1,930 km long and is the longest coral reef in the world. Crevices in reefs are good hiding places for eels, shrimps and tubeworms. The trumpetfish's snout is well adapted to searching for food deep within the crevices of the coral. Other animals eat the coral itself: the crown of thorns starfish and the parrotfish can both crunch up the coral polyps.

Hammerhead sharks

Key to coral reef

1. Green parrotfish
2. Various grunts
3. Elkhorn coral
4. Blacktip reef shark
5. Porkfish grunt
6. Crown of thorns starfish
7. Blue-striped grunts
8. Flamingo tongue
9. Soft coral polyps
10. Juvenile blue surgeon fish
11. Brittle starfish
12. Tube sponge
13. Sea urchin
14. Sea slug
15. Stinging coral
16. Trumpetfish
17. Soft coral
18. Sea fan lace coral
19. Queen angelfish
20. Queen parrotfish
21. Blue surgeonfish
22. Loggerhead turtle
23. Tubeworms
24. Four-eyed butterflyfish

The Creation of Land

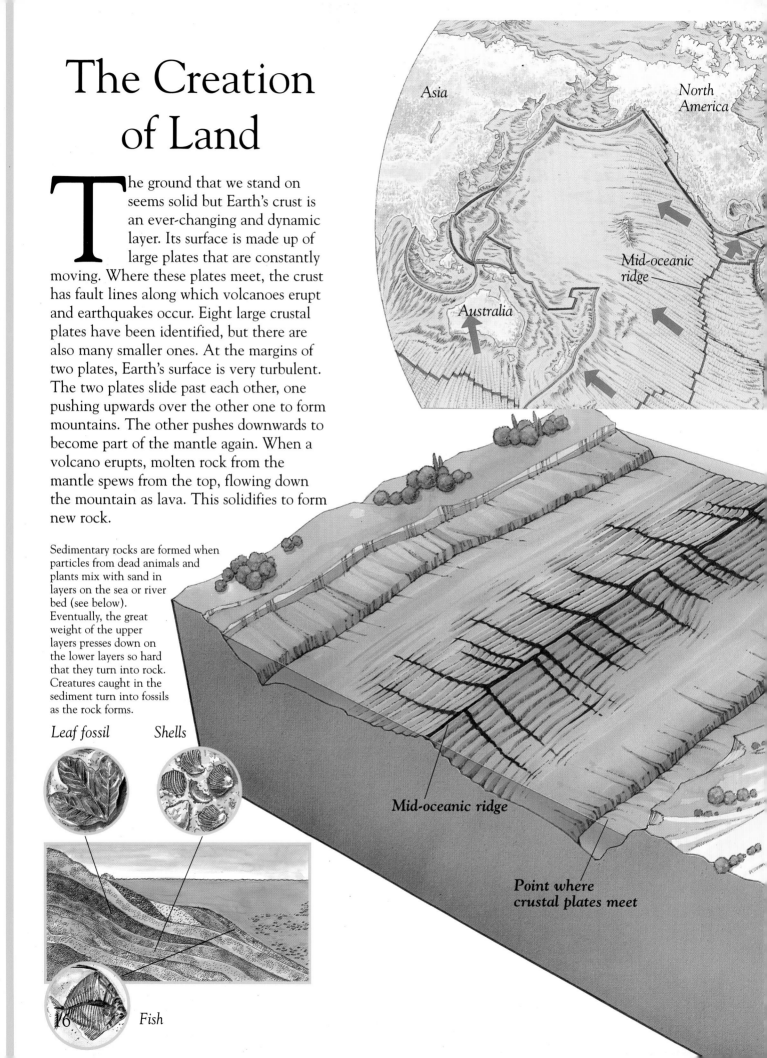

The ground that we stand on seems solid but Earth's crust is an ever-changing and dynamic layer. Its surface is made up of large plates that are constantly moving. Where these plates meet, the crust has fault lines along which volcanoes erupt and earthquakes occur. Eight large crustal plates have been identified, but there are also many smaller ones. At the margins of two plates, Earth's surface is very turbulent. The two plates slide past each other, one pushing upwards over the other one to form mountains. The other pushes downwards to become part of the mantle again. When a volcano erupts, molten rock from the mantle spews from the top, flowing down the mountain as lava. This solidifies to form new rock.

Sedimentary rocks are formed when particles from dead animals and plants mix with sand in layers on the sea or river bed (see below). Eventually, the great weight of the upper layers presses down on the lower layers so hard that they turn into rock. Creatures caught in the sediment turn into fossils as the rock forms.

Asia

North America

Mid-oceanic ridge

Australia

Mid-oceanic ridge

Point where crustal plates meet

Leaf fossil

Shells

Fish

16

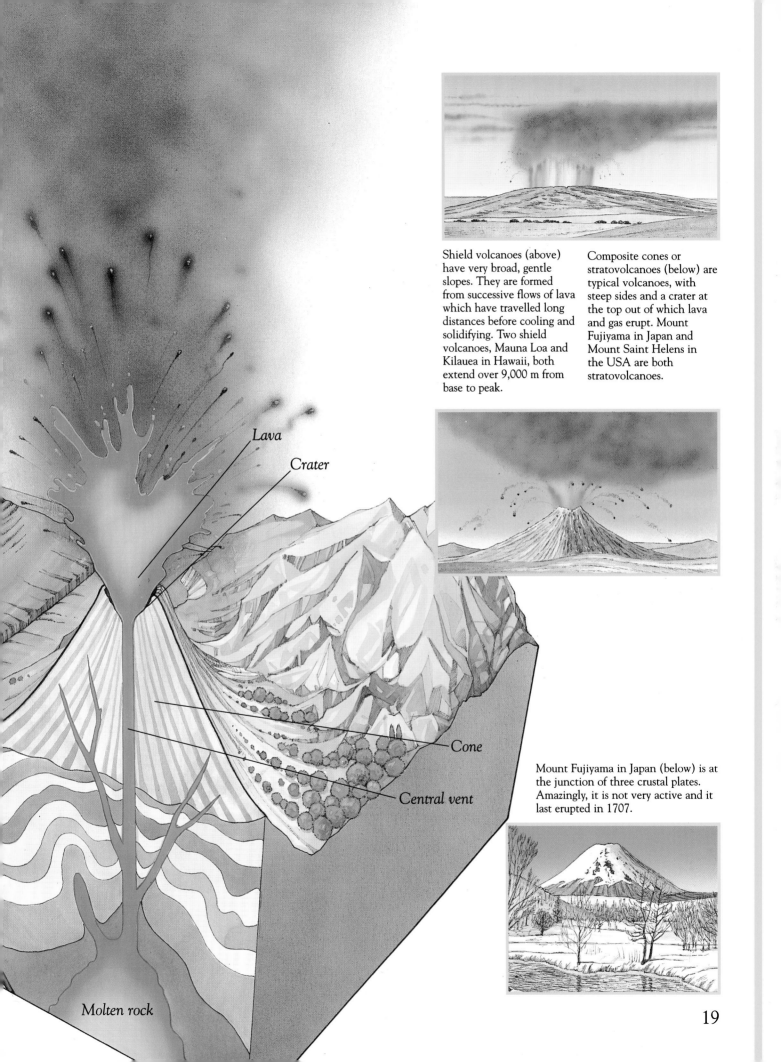

Lava

Crater

Shield volcanoes (above) have very broad, gentle slopes. They are formed from successive flows of lava which have travelled long distances before cooling and solidifying. Two shield volcanoes, Mauna Loa and Kilauea in Hawaii, both extend over 9,000 m from base to peak.

Composite cones or stratovolcanoes (below) are typical volcanoes, with steep sides and a crater at the top out of which lava and gas erupt. Mount Fujiyama in Japan and Mount Saint Helens in the USA are both stratovolcanoes.

Cone

Central vent

Mount Fujiyama in Japan (below) is at the junction of three crustal plates. Amazingly, it is not very active and it last erupted in 1707.

Molten rock

19

Extreme Environments

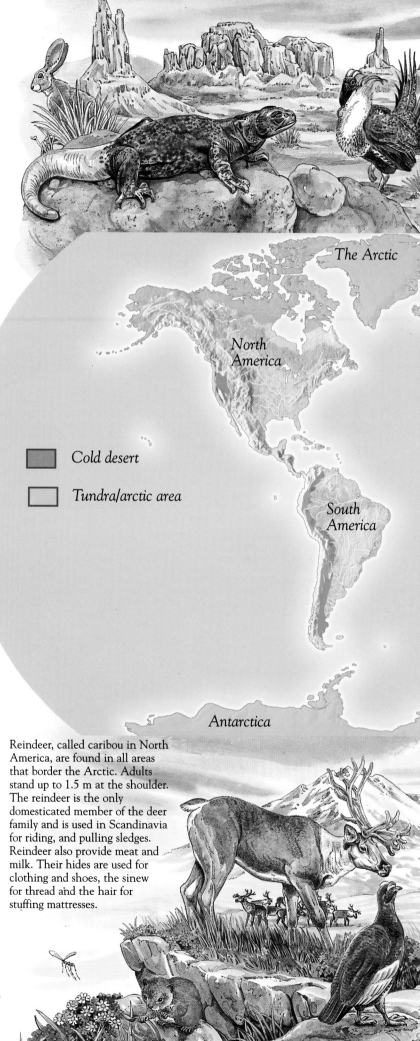

The coldest ecosystems on Earth are found at the North Pole and the South Pole. The North Pole is covered by ice all year and in winter the temperature drops to around -40°C. The South Pole is even colder and more inhospitable, with an average temperature of -50°C. It is covered by an extremely thick ice cap. Nothing can survive at the centre of the polar ice caps but some animals live at the edges (tundra) where it is a little warmer and some plants can grow. Regions of tundra are covered with shrubs, lichens and mosses and they also support several types of animal.

The Arctic

North America

☐ Cold desert

☐ Tundra/arctic area

South America

Antarctica

The polar bear's thick fur protects it from the Arctic cold. It prefers to eat seals and walrus cubs, but will also munch its way through caribou, arctic foxes, birds and shellfish. Polar bears can live for up to 25 years.

Walruses and seals are found in shallow water around the Arctic coasts. Penguins are only found in the Southern Hemisphere. Two species, the Emperor penguin and the smaller Adelie penguin are found in Antarctica.

Reindeer, called caribou in North America, are found in all areas that border the Arctic. Adults stand up to 1.5 m at the shoulder. The reindeer is the only domesticated member of the deer family and is used in Scandinavia for riding, and pulling sledges. Reindeer also provide meat and milk. Their hides are used for clothing and shoes, the sinew for thread and the hair for stuffing mattresses.

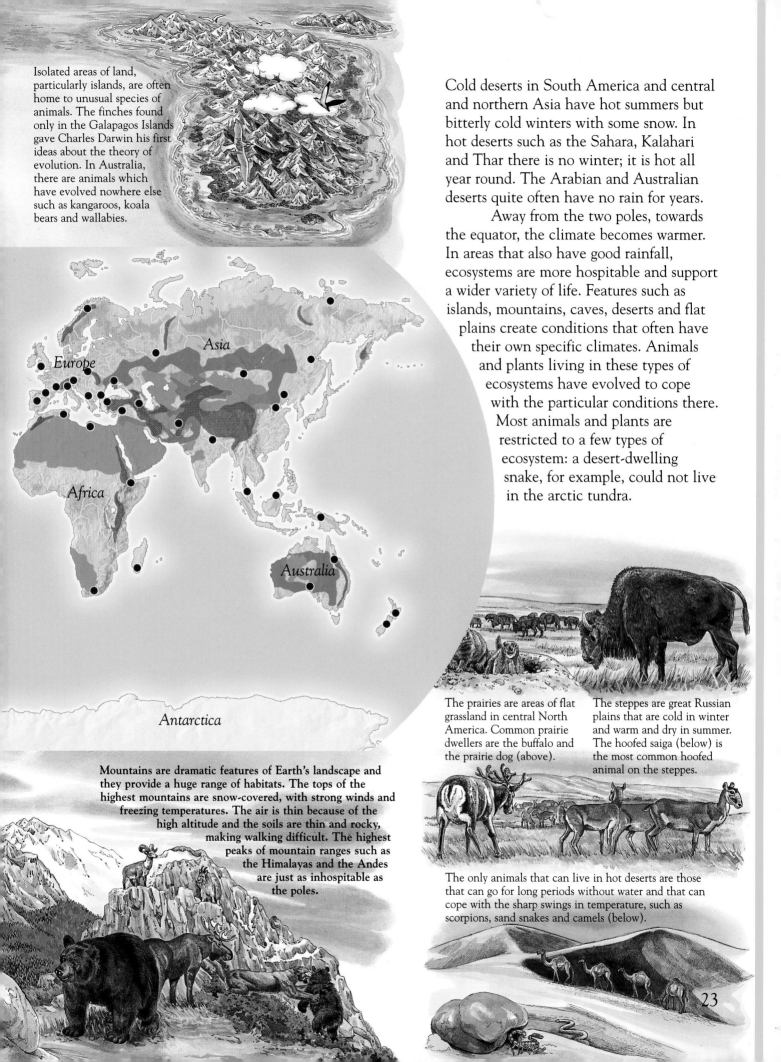

Isolated areas of land, particularly islands, are often home to unusual species of animals. The finches found only in the Galapagos Islands gave Charles Darwin his first ideas about the theory of evolution. In Australia, there are animals which have evolved nowhere else such as kangaroos, koala bears and wallabies.

Europe

Asia

Africa

Australia

Antarctica

Cold deserts in South America and central and northern Asia have hot summers but bitterly cold winters with some snow. In hot deserts such as the Sahara, Kalahari and Thar there is no winter; it is hot all year round. The Arabian and Australian deserts quite often have no rain for years.

Away from the two poles, towards the equator, the climate becomes warmer. In areas that also have good rainfall, ecosystems are more hospitable and support a wider variety of life. Features such as islands, mountains, caves, deserts and flat plains create conditions that often have their own specific climates. Animals and plants living in these types of ecosystems have evolved to cope with the particular conditions there. Most animals and plants are restricted to a few types of ecosystem: a desert-dwelling snake, for example, could not live in the arctic tundra.

The prairies are areas of flat grassland in central North America. Common prairie dwellers are the buffalo and the prairie dog (above).

The steppes are great Russian plains that are cold in winter and warm and dry in summer. The hoofed saiga (below) is the most common hoofed animal on the steppes.

The only animals that can live in hot deserts are those that can go for long periods without water and that can cope with the sharp swings in temperature, such as scorpions, sand snakes and camels (below).

Mountains are dramatic features of Earth's landscape and they provide a huge range of habitats. The tops of the highest mountains are snow-covered, with strong winds and freezing temperatures. The air is thin because of the high altitude and the soils are thin and rocky, making walking difficult. The highest peaks of mountain ranges such as the Himalayas and the Andes are just as inhospitable as the poles.

The Living Earth...

The oceans and seas cover 70% of Earth's surface with salt-water. There are also, however, regions of fresh water within the land – rivers, streams, lakes and marshes. Rivers begin as small streams of freshwater from a spring, an underground lake or melting ice on a mountain top. As each stream flows through the land, it joins up with others and they eventually form a deep river that cuts its way to the sea through soft rock and soil. Some rivers flow into deep depressions in the ground to form lakes. Swamps and marshes are permanently flooded and provide a home for many plants and animals.

Bulrushes are common in marshes all over the world and they provide shelter for creatures such as frogs and newts. The number of small animals in marshes makes them good hunting grounds for birds such as herons. The thin legs of the heron look very much like bulrush stems so the bird can stand in the shallow water and pick up a feast very easily.

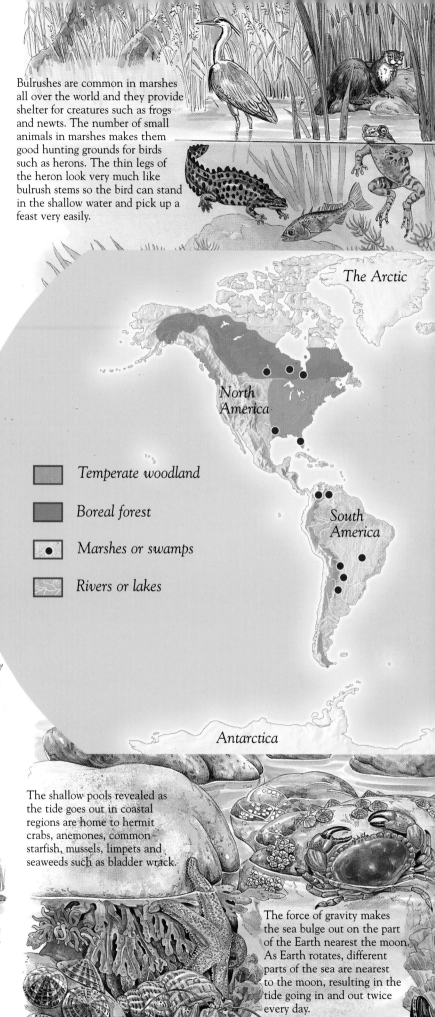

The Arctic

North America

South America

Antarctica

Temperate woodland

Boreal forest

Marshes or swamps

Rivers or lakes

The trout (above) is found in rivers across Europe. It likes to eat damselflies but has to compete with birds like swallows, that catch insects flying around close to the river surface.

Trout need fast-flowing water full of oxygen and so are not common in slow-moving lakes. Here, fish such as roach (below) thrive, because they can cope with water of almost any quality. Lakes are also home to larger insects such as the great diving beetle (below left).

The shallow pools revealed as the tide goes out in coastal regions are home to hermit crabs, anemones, common starfish, mussels, limpets and seaweeds such as bladder wrack.

The force of gravity makes the sea bulge out on the part of the Earth nearest the moon. As Earth rotates, different parts of the sea are nearest to the moon, resulting in the tide going in and out twice every day.

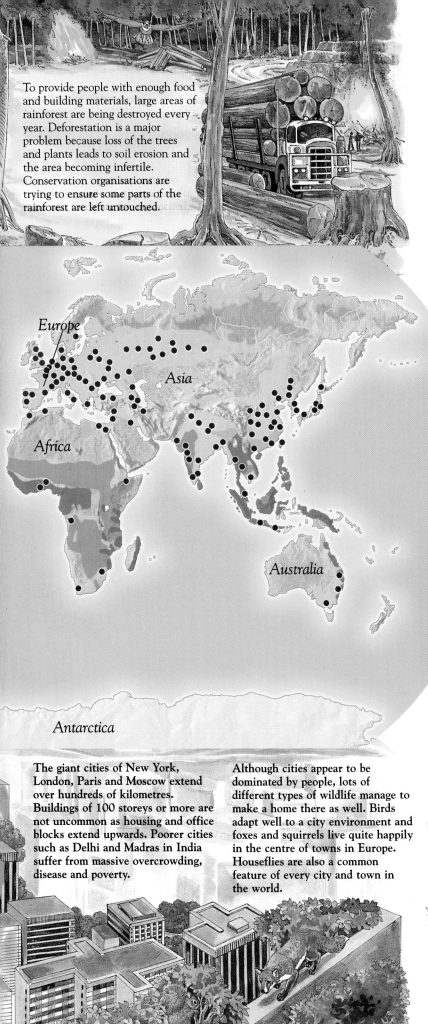

To provide people with enough food and building materials, large areas of rainforest are being destroyed every year. Deforestation is a major problem because loss of the trees and plants leads to soil erosion and the area becoming infertile. Conservation organisations are trying to ensure some parts of the rainforest are left untouched.

Europe

Asia

Africa

Australia

Antarctica

...and Humankind

All people come from a small band of African hominids that evolved about 2 million years ago. The world's population has been growing for 10,000 years and in the year 2025 will reach about 8.5 billion people. As the population grows, Earth's natural resources are becoming more scarce. Forests, grassland and rainforest are exploited, which frequently means the wildlife there loses its home and even becomes extinct. Recently, people have started to understand that we cannot keep doing this; we have to conserve species and protect their habitats.

Rainforests (above) provide the richest environments on Earth. The most species-rich plot of rainforest is in Peru, where 283 species of trees were found in one hectare.

The variety of plant food means that many different types of animal survive in the rainforest. Macaws, morpho butterflies and tree frogs are all found here.

The giant cities of New York, London, Paris and Moscow extend over hundreds of kilometres. Buildings of 100 storeys or more are not uncommon as housing and office blocks extend upwards. Poorer cities such as Delhi and Madras in India suffer from massive overcrowding, disease and poverty.

Although cities appear to be dominated by people, lots of different types of wildlife manage to make a home there as well. Birds adapt well to a city environment and foxes and squirrels live quite happily in the centre of towns in Europe. Houseflies are also a common feature of every city and town in the world.

The tropical grasslands of Africa are hot, flat plains filled with large mammals such as antelopes, gazelles and zebras. These hoofed animals themselves provide food for the predators of the savannah – the lions, tigers, cheetahs and hunting dogs. The largest mammals on Earth are also found here, including rhinoceroses, buffaloes and elephants.

The thermosphere is the deepest layer of our atmosphere. It starts at about 87 km above the ground and carries on to a height of 500 km. The temperature rises from a very chilly -100°C to scorching temperatures over 500°C. The exosphere is the upper limit of the atmosphere.

The mesosphere lies between 50 and 87 km above the ground. This is the layer in which rock fragments and debris from space burn up. The temperature falls again through this layer and at the top of the mesosphere it is barely -100°C.

The stratosphere extends from about 10 km to 50 km above Earth's surface. This is the layer in which aeroplanes fly. The conditions in the statosphere are relatively stable – there is no weather here. The temperature is constant over the first 10 km and then it rises to about 0°C at the border with the mesosphere.

The ozone layer in the stratosphere protects the Earth from damaging ultraviolet radiation that comes from the sun. The use of chemicals such as CFCs has caused a hole in the ozone layer over the South Pole that is getting bigger all the time. CFCs and other chemicals that damage the ozone layer are now banned.

The troposphere starts at the ground and ends about 10 km from the surface of the planet. This is where most weather happens. The temperature at the surface is about 20°C but at the upper end of the troposphere it is very cold, about -50°C.

This curve shows how the temperature changes throughout the atmosphere starting from Earth's surface (the bottom of the chart) and travelling up to the outermost limits of the exosphere (the top of the chart).

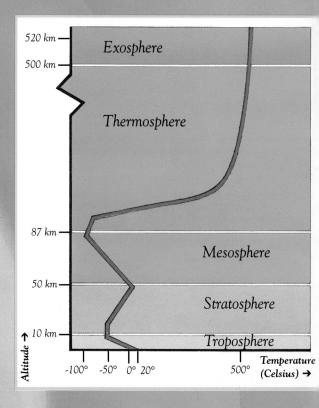

The thick clouds that form around a hurricane contain fine droplets of water that fall as heavy rain when the hurricane touches the surface of the planet.

The huge circle of clouds around a hurricane can be picked up at quite an early stage by satellite. This allows weather centres around the world to track the hurricane and warn people who are living in its path.

What an Atmosphere

Earth is surrounded by a layer of gas. This is the atmosphere and it is divided into several layers. The main layers are the troposphere, the stratosphere, the mesosphere, the thermosphere and the exosphere. The troposphere is the layer nearest the surface of the planet. Circulation of air here causes the weather patterns that can change by the hour. Weather is caused by warm and cold air travelling at different speeds, different air pressures and different amounts of moisture in the troposphere. Distinct weather patterns are found in most parts of the world. In the subtropics weather is seasonal – long, dry periods are followed by a couple of months of wet monsoons. Other parts of the world have more unpredictable weather. Extremes of weather such as hurricanes, tornadoes, cyclones and droughts are destructive and wreak havoc where they strike.

This diagram (above) shows what happens inside a hurricane. It forms as warm damp air rises and colder air is sucked in to replace it. As in a tornado, the two kinds of air start spiralling, causing a fast swirling wind that travels at high speed, reaching 350 kph in the strongest gusts. Hurricanes are very much bigger than tornadoes and can cause a lot more damage over a wider area. They have a column of warm air in the centre around which the swirling winds rotate, which is called the eye of the storm.

Monsoons (left) happen when a sudden change in wind direction causes clouds laden with water to move over warm land. This happens every year between April and October in India and Bangladesh. The rains can be torrential and can last for weeks, often resulting in flooding and loss of crops.

Tornadoes arise when banks of cold air and warm air meet. A large tornado can be 50 m across and have winds that travel at 250 kph.

Glossary

Asteroid
A rock that can be as large as 1,000 km in diameter and orbits around the sun. Most asteroids orbit in the asteroid belt between Mars and Jupiter.

Atmosphere
A layer of gas surrounding a planet or satellite.

Climate
The weather conditions typical on a particular part of Earth. The Arctic, for example, has a cold climate; tropical rainforests and deserts have hot climates.

Continent
A mass of land on Earth. There are seven of them – Asia, Africa, North America, South America, Antarctica, Europe and Australia.

Deciduous
Plants which lose their leaves in winter and grow new ones in the spring.

Density
How compact an object is. For example, lead is extremely dense but wood and materials such as polystyrene which contain lots of air pockets are much less dense.

Domesticated
Animals that have been tamed and reared by people. Common examples include cattle, sheep and pigs.

Earth's axis
This is an imaginary line drawn straight through the Earth between the North and South Poles.

Ecosystem
The physical environment and the living organisms that exist at a particular place on Earth. A desert ecosystem, for example, would include sand dunes and the camels and snakes that live on them.

Equator
An imaginary line drawn around the centre of Earth, where the planet is at its widest.

Evergreen
Plants which keep their leaves all year round.

Evolution
The process by which animals and plants change and develop over long periods of time. All life evolved from bacteria and single-celled organisms that first appeared on Earth 3,500 million years ago.

Hemisphere
A half of Earth. The equator divides the Northern and Southern hemispheres and a line passing through the North and South poles divides the Eastern and Western hemispheres.

Hominids
Ape-like animals which walk upright on two legs. Both early and modern man are hominids.

Mammal
A warm-blooded animal that gives birth to live young and feeds them with its own milk. People, lions and elephants are examples of mammals.

Mantle
The layer of molten rock that lies under Earth's crust.

Meteor
A piece of rock from space which reaches the outer limits of Earth's atmosphere, where it becomes very hot and bright and usually burns up.

Nucleus
A central cluster of particles around which others are collected. **Nuclear fission** occurs when atomic particles bind together. This causes a release of energy that is the source of energy in all stars.

Orbit
An object which travels around another object is said to be in orbit. Earth travels in an orbit around the sun.

Planet
A spherical object in space that forms from the gas and dust around a star. In our solar system, there are nine known planets, including planet Earth.

Polyp
Sea creatures which look like plants but are actually animals. All polyps have a stage in their lifecycle when they attach themselves to a rock or other hard surface under the sea. Examples of polyps are sea anemones, hydras and corals.

Reptile
A cold-blooded animal with a back bone and an internal skeleton that tends to have dry, scaly skin. Turtles, lizards, snakes, crocodiles, frogs and toads are all reptiles.

Satellite
An object that orbits around a planet. Natural satellites are moons; there are also satellites around Earth that are artificial, such as weather and communications satellites.

Savannah
Tropical grasslands.

Solar System
The system of nine known planets that orbits around our sun.

Space
The empty part of the universe that is between the planets, stars and galaxies. It contains nothing, not even gas.

Species
A group of animals who all look and behave the same and that breed together to produce young that are also the same.

Tundra
Very cold areas bordering the Arctic and Antarctic regions where only small plants can grow.

Weather
The pattern of cold, warmth, wind, rain and pressure that occurs in the stratosphere, the innermost layer of Earth's atmosphere.

Planet Earth Facts

At the equator, the diameter of Earth is 12,757 km. At the poles, where the sphere of Earth is slightly flattened, the diameter is 12,714 km.

If you flew all around the planet along the line of the equator, you would have travelled 40,075 km.

Earth has a total volume of just over 1,000 billion cubic km.

Earth's atmosphere weighs about 5 million billion tonnes but this is only 0.000088% of the total volume of the planet.

Planet Earth formed about 4,500 million years ago; life first appeared 3,500 millions years ago; the dinosaurs died out 65 million years ago and early man first appeared about 2 million years ago.

Earth is approximately 150 million km from the sun.

It takes 23.9345 hours for Earth to rotate completely and 365.256 days to orbit the sun once.

In its orbit around the sun, Earth travels at 29.79 kilometres per second.

The average surface temperature on Earth, taking into account the hottest days at the equator and the coldest nights at the South Pole, is 15°C.

Earth is the third planet from the sun in our solar system and is the only planet where life is known to exist.

Most of planet Earth is taken up by the mantle – this accounts for 84% of Earth's total volume.

Earth, including its atmosphere, weighs about 6,000 billion billion tonnes.

It takes 14,000 million years for light to reach Earth from the edge of the known universe.

Our sun is about 27,700 light years from the centre of the Milky Way.

The nearest star to the sun is Proxima Centauri, which is 4.22 light years away.

Evidence from meteors tells us that the solar system is 4,540 million years old. It probably took about 25 million years to form from gas and dust.

The hottest place on Earth is Dallol in Ethiopia, where the average temperature is 34.4°C in the shade.

Human beings are the only creatures which can survive on every continent in the world.

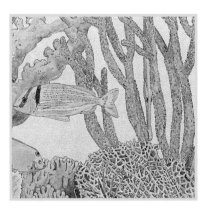

The largest desert in the world is the Sahara in North Africa., which covers an area about 8,400,000 sq km.

The driest desert in the world is the Atacama in South America; until 1971, it had not rained there for 400 years.

The deepest part of the ocean is the Marianas Trench in the Pacific. The bottom of it is 11,034 m below sea level.

The biggest active volcano in the world is Mauna Loa in Hawaii. Since 1832, it has erupted every three and a half years.

The average depth of the seas and oceans is 3,800 m. If Earth's surface was levelled out completely, it would be covered by 750 m of water.

Over 2.5 million different species of living animals are known.

The highest mountain in the world is Mount Everest, which is in the Himalayan mountain range in Asia. It is 8,848 m high.

The longest river in the world is the Nile in Egypt, which is 6,695 km long.

Ice covers more than one tenth of Earth's land surface; about three quarters of all the world's fresh water is frozen in ice sheets and glaciers.

The world's largest freshwater lake is Lake Superior. It covers an area of 82,000 sq km in the USA and Canada.

Index

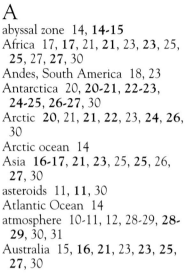

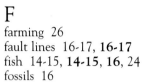
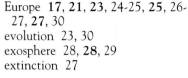
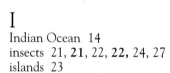

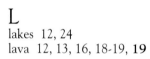